JOHN COLTRANE

For C Instruments • Transcribed Exactly from His Recorded Solos

ISBN 978-1-4584-2213-2

7777 W. BLUEMOUND RD. P.O. BOX 13819 MILWAUKEE, WI 53213

Visit Hal Leonard Online at
www.halleonard.com

JOHN COLTRANE

(1926 – 1967)

John William Coltrane, also known as "Trane," was an innovative jazz saxophonist who left an immense legacy to the jazz community. His influence on jazz, both mainstream and avant-garde, was so significant that it continues to grow to this day. He remains one of the most revered saxophonists in the history of jazz. Early in his career he played alto, later switched to tenor, and on his seventh album, MY FAVORITE THINGS, was featured playing the soprano saxophone.

One of the most distinctive aspects of Coltrane's music was the way he used chord progressions. Normally, standard "changes" move in fourths and fifths. His approach was entirely different as he instead used a series of key center movements by thirds. These third-related progressions provided Coltrane with a basis for continued experimentation with both melody and harmony. A good example of third-related progressions is found in GIANT STEPS. This sound was so identifiable that it eventually had its own name—Coltrane's Changes.

The tunes in this volume span traditional standards, such as BODY AND SOUL, BYE BYE BLACKBIRD and ALL OR NOTHING AT ALL, to Coltrane's own compositions, like the hauntingly beautiful ballad NAIMA, to the straight ahead, up tempo GIANT STEPS and IMPRESSIONS.

You'll find these helpful features in this "omni" volume:

- More than 50 note-for-note transcriptions
- Meticulous, easy-to-read notation
- Chord symbols to facilitate analyzing the solos and to provide a basis for accompaniment
- Rehearsal letters
- The recording from which each tune was transcribed included with the song title
- Rhythmic styles with metronome marks
- Specific playing techniques such as hum, split tone, and growl, to name a few

John Coltrane is an iconic figure of 20th century jazz. His playing and compositions have continued to inspire generations of jazz players throughout the world.

Acknowledgement

(A Love Supreme, Part 1)
from "A Love Supreme" MCA/Impulse! MCAD - 5660
By John Coltrane

Repeat 3 times

Ⓒ Fm11

(Vocal)

Fm11

A love su - preme, __ a love su - preme, __ a

Ⓓ

Repeat 7 times E♭m11

love su - preme, __ a love su - preme, __ a

love su - preme, __ a love su - preme, __ a love su - preme. __

Ⓔ

30

Airegin

from *Cookin' with the Miles Davis Quintet (Miles Davis) Prestige OJCCD-128-2*

By Sonny Rollins

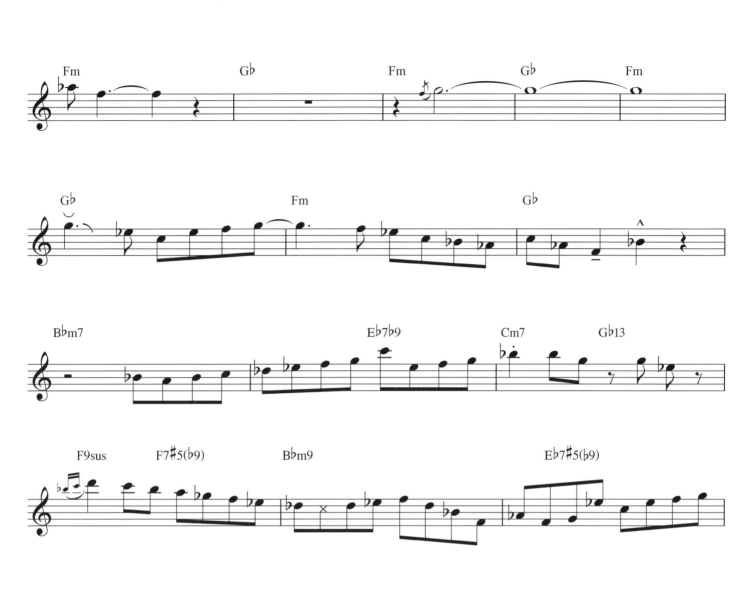

Alabama

from *"Coltrane Live at Birdland"* MCA/Impulse! A - 49

By John Coltrane

All Blues

from "Kind Of Blue" (Miles Davis) CBS 40579

By Miles Davis

All or Nothing at All

from *Ballads MCA/Impulse - 29012*

Words by Jack Lawrence
Music by Arthur Altman

Medium Latin (♩ = 176)

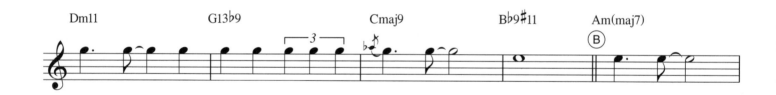

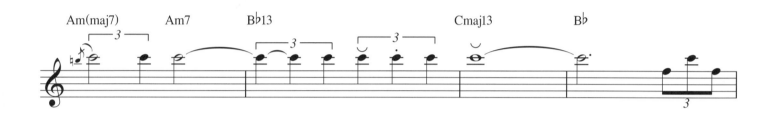

25   **Fadeout**

Bessie's Blues
from *"Crescent" IMPULSE AS-66*
By John Coltrane

Blue Train

(a/k/a BLUE TRANE)
from *"Blue Train"* BLUE NOTE BST 81577
By John Coltrane

Body and Soul
from *"Coltrane's Sound"* SD 1419
Words by Edward Heyman, Robert Sour and Frank Eyton
Music by John Green

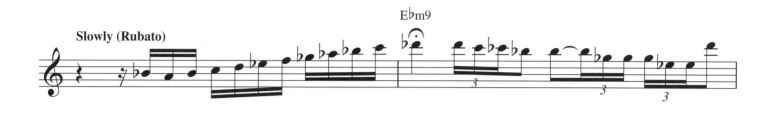

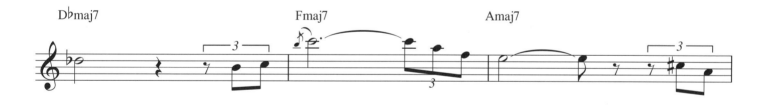

By the Numbers
from *"The Last Trane"* Prestige 7378
By John Coltrane

Bye Bye Blackbird

from 'Round About Midnight (Miles Davis) Columbia CK 85201
Lyric by Mort Dixon
Music by Ray Henderson

D Trumpet Solo

64

E Fmaj9 *(John Coltrane)* C9sus Fmaj9

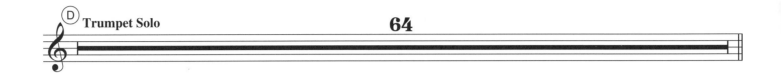

C9sus C7#5(♭9) F6 A♭m7

Gm7 Am7 D7#9

Gm7 C9sus Gm7♭5 D7♭9

Gm7 D7♭9 Gm7

C13sus C7#5(♭9) Fmaj9

47

Cattin'

from *Cattin' With Coltrane and Quinichette Prestige OJC-7158*

By Mal Waldron

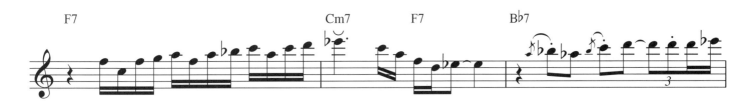

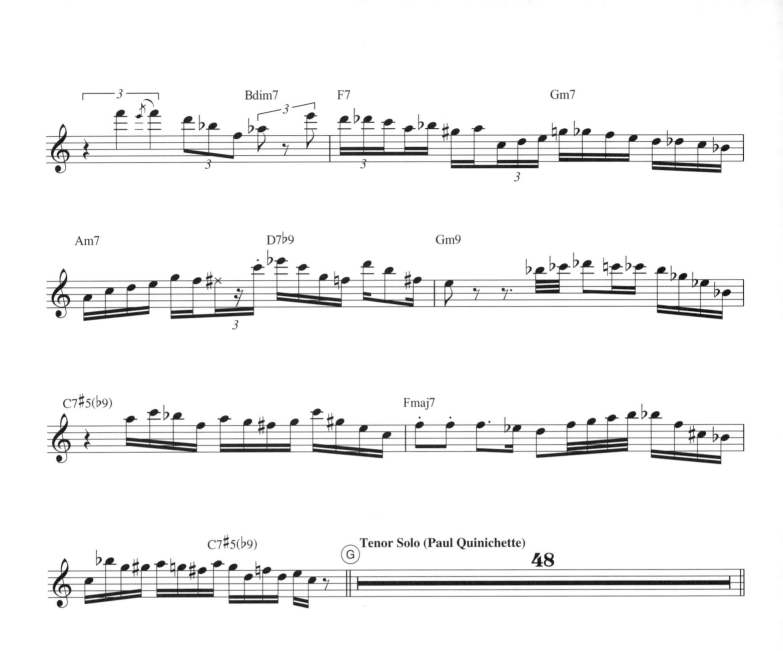

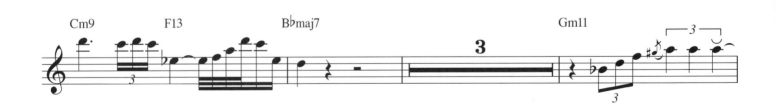

Chasin' the Trane

from *"Live at the Village Vanguard" Impulse! IMPD-251*

By John Coltrane

Most of Coltrane's false fingerings in this solo are played a fifth below pitch unless indicated otherwise.

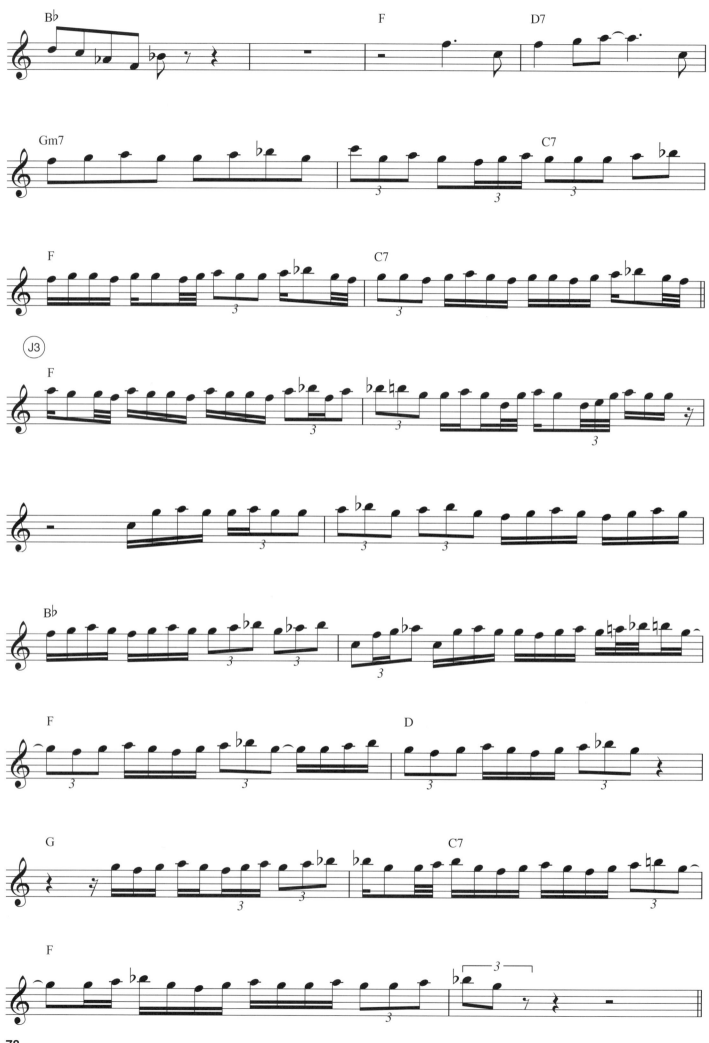

Central Park West

from *"Best of John Coltrane"* ATLANTIC SD 1541

By John Coltrane

Countdown
from *"Giant Steps"* ATLANTIC SD 1311
By John Coltrane

Played as C, overtone sounds as G

Cousin Mary

from *"Giant Steps"* ATLANTIC SD 1311

By John Coltrane

Crescent

from *"Crescent"* IMPULSE AS-66
By John Coltrane

Eclypso
from *"The Cats"* New Jazz 8217
By Tommy Flanagan

Fine

Equinox
from *"Best of John Coltrane"* ATLANTIC SD 1541
By John Coltrane

Giant Steps

from *"Giant Steps"* ATLANTIC SD 1311

By John Coltrane

Played as C, overtone sounds as G

119

Goldsboro Express
from *"Bahia"* Prestige PR 7353
By John Coltrane

Grand Central

from *"Cannonball Adderley Quintet in Chicago"* MERCURY MG 20499

By John Coltrane

Impressions

from *"Coltranology-Volume One"* AFFINITY 32-2051

By John Coltrane

In a Sentimental Mood

from *"Duke Ellington & John Coltrane" Impulse! MCAD-39103*

Words and Music by Duke Ellington, Irving Mills and Manny Kurtz

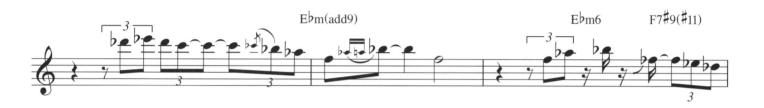

142

India

from *"Impressions"* Impulse! 314 543 416 -2

By John Coltrane

148

(Lip down)

Bass Clarinet Solo

158

(Hum)

(Coltrane drops a beat)

Lazy Bird
from "*Blue Train*" *BLUE NOTE BST 81577*

By John Coltrane

Just for the Love

from *"Whims of Chambers"* Blue Note 37647

By John Coltrane

Like Sonny
(Simple Like)
from "*Alternate Takes*" ATLANTIC 1668
By John Coltrane

Lonnie's Lament

from *"Crescent"* IMPULSE AS-66

By John Coltrane

Locomotion

from "*Blue Train*" *BLUE NOTE BST 81577*
By John Coltrane

Lush Life

from *"John Coltrane & Johnny Hartman" Impulse! MCAD-5661*

By Billy Strayhorn

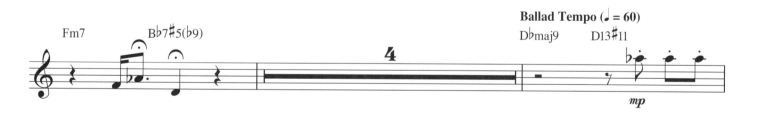

Mary's Blues
from *"Dakar" Prestige PR 7280*
By Pepper Adams

Mr. P.C.
from "Giant Steps" ATLANTIC SD 1311
By John Coltrane

Moment's Notice

from "*Blue Train*" *BLUE NOTE BST 81577*

By John Coltrane

195

My Favorite Things

from "Best of John Coltrane" ATLANTIC SD 1541

Lyrics by Oscar Hammerstein II
Music by Richard Rodgers

200

203

My One and Only Love

from *"John Coltrane and Johnny Hartman"* MCA/Impulse! MCAD-5661
Words by Robert Mellin
Music by Guy Wood

Nita

from *"Whims of Chambers"* Blue Note 37647
By John Coltrane

Naima

from *"Alternate Takes" ATLANTIC 1668*

By John Coltrane

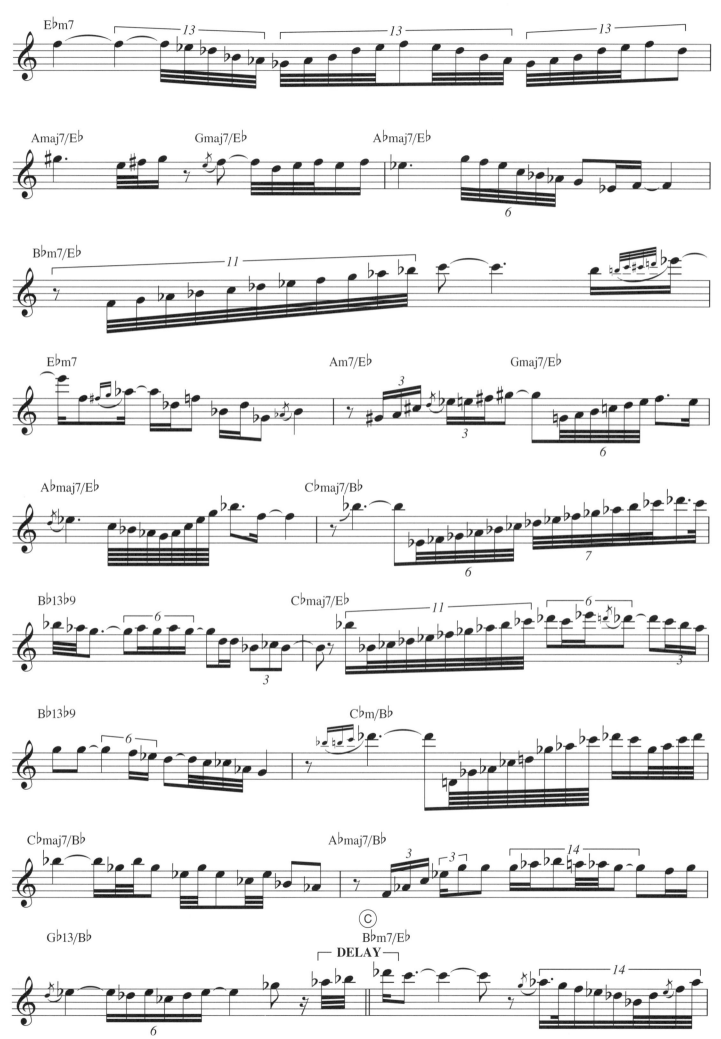

Oleo

from *"Jazz At The Plaza"* (Miles Davis) COLOMBIA 32470
By Sonny Rollins

217

*Played as Db, overtone sounds as Ab
**Played as C, overtone sounds as G

218

221

Omicron
from "Whims of Chambers" Blue Note 37647
By Donald Byrd

Paul's Pal

from "The Ray Draper Quintet feat. John Coltrane" New Jazz 8228

By Sonny Rollins

Pursuance
(Part III)
from *"A Love Supreme"* IMPULSE AS-66
By John Coltrane

Russian Lullaby

from *"Soultrane"* Prestige 7142
Words and Music by Irving Berlin

So What

from *"Kind Of Blue" (Miles Davis) CBS 40579*
By Miles Davis

Softly as in a Morning Sunrise

from "*John Coltrane Live at the Village Vanguard*" *Impulse! IMPD-251*

Lyrics by Oscar Hammerstein II
Music by Sigmund Romberg

Some Other Blues
from *"Coltrane Jazz"* ATLANTIC CS 1354
By John Coltrane

*During the solo the band is playing standard blues changes.

Spiral
from *"Giant Steps"* ATLANTIC SD 1311
By John Coltrane

Played as D♭, overtone sounds as A♭

Syeeda's Song Flute

from *"Giant Steps"* ATLANTIC SD 1311

By John Coltrane

Theme for Ernie

from *"Soultrane"* Prestige 7142 (OJC-021)

By Fred Lacey

267

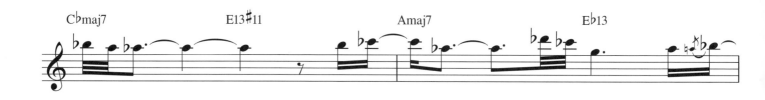

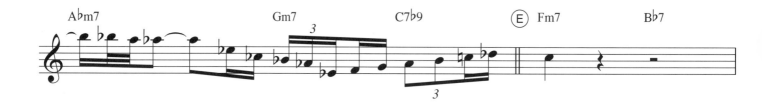

Piano Solo

14

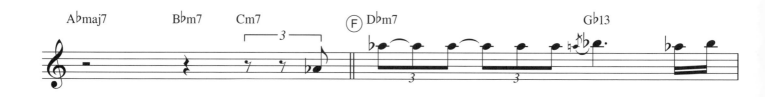

26 - 2
from *Coltrane's Sound (Bonus Track) Atlantic SD 1419*
By John Coltrane

Velvet Scene
from "Dakar" Prestige PR 7280
By Mal Waldron

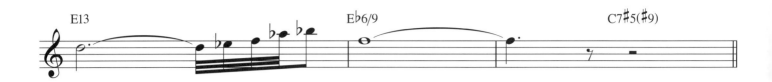

We Six

from *"Whims of Chambers"* Blue Note BST-81534

By Donald Byrd

Witches Pit
from "Dakar" Prestige PR 7280
By Pepper Adams

JOHN COLTRANE
Collections

JOHN COLTRANE – OMNIBOOK
More than 50 Coltrane classics, transcribed exactly from his recorded solos. Includes: All Blues • Blue Train (Blue Trane) • Body and Soul • Bye Bye Blackbird • Countdown • Cousin Mary • Giant Steps • Impressions • India • Lazy Bird • Lush Life • Mr. P.C. • Moment's Notice • My Favorite Things • Naima (Niema) • Spiral • Syeeda's Song Flute • Witches Pit • and more.
00307391 B-Flat Instruments $19.99
00307392 E-Flat Instruments $24.99
00307393 C Instruments $24.99
00307394 Bass Clef Instruments $24.99

THE BEST OF JOHN COLTRANE
A Step-by-Step Breakdown of the Sax Styles & Techniques of a Jazz Legend
Book/CD Pack
This book/CD pack will teach saxophonists 12 of Coltrane's signature licks, including ones from: Blue Train (Blue Trane) • Bye Bye Blackbird • Giant Steps • Impressions • Moment's Notice • My Favorite Things • Naima (Niema) • and more. Features in-depth analysis of his solos and compositions.
00695826 Saxophone $19.99

JOHN COLTRANE PLAYS "COLTRANE CHANGES"
transcribed by Masaya Yamaguchi
foreword by David Demsey
In the late 1950s, John Coltrane composed or arranged a series of tunes that used chord progressions based on a series of key center movements by thirds, rather than the usual fourths and fifths of standard progressions. This sound is so aurally identifiable and has received so much attention from jazz musicians that it has become known as "Coltrane's Changes." This book presents an exploration of his changes by studying 13 of his arrangements, each containing Coltrane's unique harmonic formula. It includes complete solo transcriptions with extensive performance notes for each. Titles include: Body and Soul • But Not for Me • Central Park West • Countdown • Fifth House • Giant Steps • Summertime • and more.
00672493 Saxophone $19.95

JOHN COLTRANE – GIANT STEPS
Artist Transcriptions
This timeless album is considered by many to be the most influential jazz recording of its time. Features note-for-note transcriptions of these classics: Countdown • Cousin Mary • Giant Steps • Mr. P.C. • Naima • Spiral • Syeeda's Song Flute.
00672529 Tenor Saxophone $14.99

JOHN COLTRANE PLAYS "GIANT STEPS"
transcriptions and analysis by David Demsey
This historical editon includes complete transcriptions of every recorded solo by jazz master John Coltrane on his legendary composition "Giant Steps" – all 96 choruses! It also includes analysis of the tune and solos, historical background and previously unpublished photos from the period, and more, making it a collector's item as well as an important practice and learning tool.
00672349 Tenor Saxophone $19.95

JOHN COLTRANE – A LOVE SUPREME
The *All Music Guide* calls John Coltrane's *A Love Supreme* "easily one of the most important records ever made," and Coltrane has referred to it as his "gift to God." This exceptional songbook presents exact note-for-note tenor saxophone transcriptions for every piece on this landmark album. Includes: Acknowledgement (Part I) • Resolution (Part II) • Pursuance (Part III) • Psalm (Part IV).
00672494 Tenor Saxophone $14.95

THE MUSIC OF JOHN COLTRANE
This collection includes over 100 Coltrane classics: Acknowledgement (Part 1) • Bessie's Blues • Blue Train (Blue Trane) • Chasin' the Trane • Evolution • Giant Steps • Impressions • Lonnie's Lament • Mr. P.C. • Naima (Niema) • Some Other Blues • Venus • Village Blues • and more.
00660165 Tenor Saxophone $22.95

JOHN COLTRANE SOLOS
This collection of 26 tenor sax transcriptions features some of jazz giant John Coltane's most important solos: Blue Train • Central Part West • Giant Steps • Impressions • Lazy Bird • Moment's Notice • My Favorite Things • 'Round Midnight • and more. Includes a bio, notation guide, alternate fingerings, and discography with historical notes on the recordings.
00673233 Soprano and Tenor Saxophone $22.95

JOHN COLTRANE – JAZZ PLAY-ALONG VOL. 13
Book/CD Pack
The Jazz Play-Along series is the ultimate learning tool for all jazz musicians. With musician-friendly lead sheets, melody cues, and other split-track choices on the included CD, this first-of-its-kind package makes learning to play jazz easier than ever before. For study, each tune includes a split track with: • Melody cue with proper style and inflection • Professional rhythm tracks • Choruses for soloing • Removable bass part • Removable piano part. For performance, each tune also has: • An additional full stereo accompaniment track (no melody) • Additional choruses for soloing. Includes: Blue Train (Blue Trane) • Countdown • Cousin Mary • Equinox • Giant Steps • Impressions • Lazy Bird • Mr. P.C. • Moment's Notice • Naima (Neima).
00843006 B♭, E♭, C, and Bass Clef Instruments $16.95

Prices, content, and availability subject to change without notice.

HAL•LEONARD® CORPORATION
7777 W. BLUEMOUND RD. P.O. BOX 13819 MILWAUKEE, WI 53213

www.halleonard.com

0513

The Best-Selling Jazz Book of All Time Is Now Legal!

The Real Books are the most popular jazz books of all time. Since the 1970s, musicians have trusted these volumes to get them through every gig, night after night. The problem is that the books were illegally produced and distributed, without any regard to copyright law, or royalties paid to the composers who created these musical masterpieces.

Hal Leonard is very proud to present the first legitimate and legal editions of these books ever produced. You won't even notice the difference, other than all the notorious errors being fixed: the covers and typeface look the same, the song lists are nearly identical, and the price for our edition is even cheaper than the originals!

Every conscientious musician will appreciate that these books are now produced accurately and ethically, benefitting the songwriters that we owe for some of the greatest tunes of all time!

VOLUME 1
00240221	C Edition	$35.00
00240224	B♭ Edition	$35.00
00240225	E♭ Edition	$35.00
00240226	Bass Clef Edition	$35.00
00240292	C Edition 6 x 9	$30.00
00240339	B♭ Edition 6 x 9	$30.00
00451087	C Edition on CD-ROM	$25.00
00240302	A-D CD Backing Tracks	$24.99
00240303	E-J CD Backing Tracks	$24.95
00240304	L-R CD Backing Tracks	$24.95
00240305	S-Z CD Backing Tracks	$24.99
00110604	Book/USB Flash Drive Backing Tracks Pack	$79.99
00110599	USB Flash Drive Only	$50.00

VOLUME 2
00240222	C Edition	$35.50
00240227	B♭ Edition	$35.00
00240228	E♭ Edition	$35.00
00240229	Bass Clef Edition	$35.00
00240293	C Edition 6 x 9	$30.00
00451088	C Edition on CD-ROM	$27.99
00240351	A-D CD Backing Tracks	$24.99
00240352	E-I CD Backing Tracks	$24.99
00240353	J-R CD Backing Tracks	$24.99
00240354	S-Z CD Backing Tracks	$24.99

VOLUME 3
00240233	C Edition	$35.00
00240284	B♭ Edition	$35.00
00240285	E♭ Edition	$35.00
00240286	Bass Clef Edition	$35.00
00240338	C Edition 6 x 9	$30.00
00451089	C Edition on CD-ROM	$29.99

VOLUME 4
00240296	C Edition	$35.00
00103348	B♭ Edition	$35.00
00103349	E♭ Edition	$35.00
00103350	Bass Clef Edition	$35.00

VOLUME 5
00240349	C Edition	$35.00

Also available:
00240264	The Real Blues Book	$34.99
00310910	The Real Bluegrass Book	$29.99
00240137	Miles Davis Real Book	$19.95
00240355	The Real Dixieland Book	$29.99
00240235	The Duke Ellington Real Book	$19.99
00240348	The Real Latin Book	$35.00
00240358	The Charlie Parker Real Book	$19.99
00240331	The Bud Powell Real Book	$19.99
00240313	The Real Rock Book	$35.00
00240323	The Real Rock Book – Vol. 2	$35.00
00240359	The Real Tab Book – Vol. 1	$32.50
00240317	The Real Worship Book	$29.99

THE REAL CHRISTMAS BOOK
00240306	C Edition	$29.99
00240345	B♭ Edition	$29.99
00240346	E♭ Edition	$29.99
00240347	Bass Clef Edition	$29.99
00240431	A-G CD Backing Tracks	$24.99
00240432	H-M CD Backing Tracks	$24.99
00240433	N-Y CD Backing Tracks	$24.99

THE REAL VOCAL BOOK
00240230	Volume 1 High Voice	$35.00
00240307	Volume 1 Low Voice	$35.00
00240231	Volume 2 High Voice	$35.00
00240308	Volume 2 Low Voice	$35.00
00240391	Volume 3 High Voice	$35.00
00240392	Volume 3 Low Voice	$35.00

THE REAL BOOK – STAFF PAPER
00240327		$10.99

HOW TO PLAY FROM A REAL BOOK
FOR ALL MUSICIANS
by Robert Rawlins
00312097		$17.50

Complete song lists online
at www.halleonard.com
Prices, content, and availability subject to change without notice.

HAL•LEONARD® CORPORATION
7777 W. BLUEMOUND RD. P.O. BOX 13819 MILWAUKEE, WI 53213

1113

Jazz Instruction & Improvisation

BOOKS FOR ALL INSTRUMENTS FROM HAL LEONARD

AN APPROACH TO JAZZ IMPROVISATION
by Dave Pozzi
Musicians Institute Press
Explore the styles of Charlie Parker, Sonny Rollins, Bud Powell and others with this comprehensive guide to jazz improvisation. Covers: scale choices • chord analysis • phrasing • melodies • harmonic progressions • more.
00695135 Book/CD Pack......................................$17.95

THE ART OF MODULATING
FOR PIANISTS AND JAZZ MUSICIANS
by Carlos Salzedo &
Lucile Lawrence
Schirmer
The Art of Modulating is a treatise originally intended for the harp, but this edition has been edited for use by intermediate keyboardists and other musicians who have an understanding of basic music theory. In its pages you will find: table of intervals; modulation rules; modulation formulas; examples of modulation; extensions and cadences; ten fragments of dances; five characteristic pieces; and more.
50490581 ....$19.99

BUILDING A JAZZ VOCABULARY
By Mike Steinel
A valuable resource for learning the basics of jazz from Mike Steinel of the University of North Texas. It covers: the basics of jazz • how to build effective solos • a comprehensive practice routine • and a jazz vocabulary of the masters.
00849911 ....$19.95

THE CYCLE OF FIFTHS
by Emile and Laura De Cosmo
This essential instruction book provides more than 450 exercises, including hundreds of melodic and rhythmic ideas. The book is designed to help improvisors master the cycle of fifths, one of the primary progressions in music. Guaranteed to refine technique, enhance improvisational fluency, and improve sight-reading!
00311114 ....$16.99

THE DIATONIC CYCLE
by Emile and Laura De Cosmo
Renowned jazz educators Emile and Laura De Cosmo provide more than 300 exercises to help improvisors tackle one of music's most common progressions: the diatonic cycle. This book is guaranteed to refine technique, enhance improvisational fluency, and improve sight-reading!
00311115 ....$16.95

EAR TRAINING
by Keith Wyatt,
Carl Schroeder and Joe Elliott
Musicians Institute Press
Covers: basic pitch matching • singing major and minor scales • identifying intervals • transcribing melodies and rhythm • identifying chords and progressions • seventh chords and the blues • modal interchange, chromaticism, modulation • and more.
00695198 Book/2-CD Pack $24.95

EXERCISES AND ETUDES FOR THE JAZZ INSTRUMENTALIST
by J.J. Johnson
Designed as study material and playable by any instrument, these pieces run the gamut of the jazz experience, featuring common and uncommon time signatures and keys, and styles from ballads to funk. They are progressively graded so that both beginners and professionals will be challenged by the demands of this wonderful music.
00842018 Bass Clef Edition $16.95
00842042 Treble Clef Edition $16.95

JAZZOLOGY
THE ENCYCLOPEDIA OF JAZZ THEORY FOR ALL MUSICIANS
by Robert Rawlins and
Nor Eddine Bahha
This comprehensive resource covers a variety of jazz topics, for beginners and pros of any instrument. The book serves as an encyclopedia for reference, a thorough methodology for the student, and a workbook for the classroom.
00311167 ....$19.99

JAZZ THEORY RESOURCES
by Bert Ligon
Houston Publishing, Inc.
This is a jazz theory text in two volumes. **Volume 1 includes**: review of basic theory • rhythm in jazz performance • triadic generalization • diatonic harmonic progressions and analysis • substitutions and turnarounds • and more. **Volume 2 includes**: modes and modal frameworks • quartal harmony • extended tertian structures and triadic superimposition • pentatonic applications • coloring "outside" the lines and beyond • and more.
00030458 Volume 1 ....$39.95
00030459 Volume 2 ....$29.95

JOY OF IMPROV
by Dave Frank
and John Amaral
This book/CD course on improvisation for all instruments and all styles will help players develop monster musical skills! Book One imparts a solid basis in technique, rhythm, chord theory, ear training and improv concepts. **Book Two** explores more advanced chord voicings, chord arranging techniques and more challenging blues and melodic lines. The CD can be used as a listening and play-along tool.
00220005 Book 1 – Book/CD Pack.......................$27.99
00220006 Book 2 – Book/CD Pack.......................$26.99

THE PATH TO JAZZ IMPROVISATION
by Emile and Laura De Cosmo
This fascinating jazz instruction book offers an innovative, scholarly approach to the art of improvisation. It includes in-depth analysis and lessons about: cycle of fifths • diatonic cycle • overtone series • pentatonic scale • harmonic and melodic minor scale • polytonal order of keys • blues and bebop scales • modes • and more.
00310904 ....$14.99

THE SOURCE
THE DICTIONARY OF CONTEMPORARY AND TRADITIONAL SCALES
by Steve Barta
This book serves as an informative guide for people who are looking for good, solid information regarding scales, chords, and how they work together. It provides right and left hand fingerings for scales, chords, and complete inversions. Includes over 20 different scales, each written in all 12 keys.
00240885 ....$18.99

21 BEBOP EXERCISES
by Steve Rawlins
This book/CD pack is both a warm-up collection and a manual for bebop phrasing. Its tasty and sophisticated exercises will help you develop your proficiency with jazz interpretation. It concentrates on practice in all twelve keys – moving higher by half-step – to help develop dexterity and range. The companion CD includes all of the exercises in 12 keys.
00315341 Book/CD Pack....................................$17.95

HAL•LEONARD®
CORPORATION
7777 W. BLUEMOUND RD. P.O. BOX 13819 MILWAUKEE, WI 53213

Visit Hal Leonard online at
www.halleonard.com

Prices, contents & availability
subject to change without notice.